Saving Animals with Science

Saving Endangered Species

Tracy Sue Walker

Lerner Publications ◆ Minneapolis

For Catherine and Leo Gentile

Lerner Publications Company
An imprint of Lerner Publishing Group, Inc.
241 First Avenue North
Minneapolis, MN 55401 USA

For reading levels and more information, look up this title
at www.lernerbooks.com.

Main body text set in Adrianna Regular.
Typeface provided by Chank.

Library of Congress Cataloging-in-Publication Data

Names: Walker, Tracy Sue, author.
Title: Saving endangered species / Tracy Sue Walker.
Description: Minneapolis : Lerner Publications, [2024] | Series: Searchlight books - saving animals with science | Includes bibliographical references and index. | Audience: Ages 8–11 | Audience: Grades 4–6 | Summary: "Thousands of animals are endangered. Scientists are working to save these species through captive breeding and releasing the animals into the wild. Young readers discover practical ways they can help animals in their community"— Provided by publisher.
Identifiers: LCCN 2023014572 (print) | LCCN 2023014573 (ebook) | ISBN 9798765609149 (library binding) | ISBN 9798765624791 (paperback) | ISBN 9798765617304 (epub)
Subjects: LCSH: Endangered species—Conservation—Juvenile literature. | Biodiversity conservation—Juvenile literature. | Ecosystem management—Juvenile literature. | BISAC: JUVENILE NONFICTION / Animals / Animal Welfare
Classification: LCC QH75 .W345 2024 (print) | LCC QH75 (ebook) | DDC 333.95/16—dc23/eng/20230515

LC record available at https://lccn.loc.gov/2023014572
LC ebook record available at https://lccn.loc.gov/2023014573

Manufactured in the United States of America
1-1009623-51592-6/27/2023

Table of Contents

Chapter 1

PROTECTING ANIMALS

In 2021, Chinese officials made an exciting announcement. They said giant pandas were no longer considered endangered—at very high risk of dying out.

The officials said the giant pandas were considered vulnerable instead. Although they were still at risk of dying out, the population in the wild had increased. Scientists worked hard for years to help giant pandas.

About nineteen hundred giant pandas were in the wild in 2022.

Protecting natural habitats was one of the most important parts of their work. The rising number of giant pandas brought hope for other endangered species too.

A scientist studies a habitat.

Endangered Status

Scientists look at several things to decide if a species is endangered. Habitat is one factor. Some animals' habitats are getting smaller. This can happen because people cut down trees or use the area for housing or farming. When there are fewer or smaller habitats, it is harder for animals to live and have babies. Scientists also study the population. They see how many of a certain type of animal there are and how that number has changed over time. They might also look at the dangers the animal faces, from natural predators to humans who hunt them.

Climate change is making temperatures rise. This is causing animals to lose their habitats. For example, warmer temperatures are causing icebergs to melt, which leaves fewer places for polar bears to live.

Melting icebergs

This power plant burns coal to make energy.

Burning fossil fuels is the main cause of climate change. Some fossil fuels, such as oil and coal, are used in manufacturing and transportation. But people can help solve climate problems by using more green energy such as from the wind and sun.

Spotlight On
Rebecca Shaw

Rebecca Shaw serves as chief scientist and senior vice president at the World Wildlife Fund. She works with scientists and researchers to identify new challenges to endangered animals. Then Shaw and the experts work together to come up with ways to help animals. She has been a leader in conservation and climate change research for over thirty years.

Chapter 2

TECHNOLOGY TO THE RESCUE

People use technology to help protect endangered animals. Technology can do some jobs better and faster than humans.

Counting on Technology

Scientists need to keep track of how many animals are in the wild to know if a group is endangered. But it's hard for people to count animals. The animals might hide, or people might count the same animal twice.

Researchers use drones to help count animals.

Drones can fly above areas that might be hard for people to get to. Animals are also less likely to hide from drones. Some drones take pictures so researchers can then count the number of animals from these images. Other drones use software to count and provide that data.

A DRONE FLIES ABOVE HILLS.

A satellite is a machine that is sent into space and moves around something such as a planet or moon.

Out of this World

Some satellites can collect almost 2,000 square miles (5,180 sq. km) of images every few minutes. Like drones, they make counting animals faster and easier. What might take humans weeks or months can be done by satellites in a matter of days. They're more accurate too.

Deep Dive
Artificial Intelligence

Artificial intelligence (AI) is a type of technology that gives machines the ability to seem as if they have human intelligence. AI can do some jobs faster and more accurately than people. Scientists are using AI to help them save endangered animals.

Conservationists record animals in a tracker.

AI Saving Animals

AI can be used for camera surveillance and satellite communications. This technology provides almost instant images that help scientists. For example, a surveillance camera can photograph a poacher in action and send a notice to a park ranger. The ranger can then act immediately. With AI, researchers can stop poachers, track water loss, and count populations faster and with greater accuracy than ever before.

Chapter 3

HOW BIOLOGY SAVES ENDANGERED SPECIES

Scientists have discovered ways to help protect endangered species and the environment. Stopping the spread of non-native species, such as Burmese pythons in the Everglades, is one way. Captive breeding is another.

Stopping Invasive Species

Non-native species can be bad for natural habitats and the animals that live there. Such species are also called invasive species. Some can harm native animals and cause them to become endangered. Invasive species can enter a habitat in many ways. Shipping goods across oceans and land is one way species come to a new habitat.

Burmese pythons are not native to Florida. They might have been introduced there when a pet python escaped or was released.

Spotted lantern flies are an invasive species. They kill trees and other plants.

Invasive species can eat the food that native animals depend on. They can destroy plant life that provides shelter and food. Invasive species often eat native animals. This causes the native animal population to decrease. Preventing invasive species from moving into a habitat is the best way to battle the problem.

There are many ways scientists try to stop the spread of invasive species. They watch habitats closely for any signs of non-native animals or plants. They educate the public about their dangers. Scientists also try to remove invasive species.

Scientists look at bark to learn more about the bugs that live there.

Captive Breeding

Sometimes scientists take endangered animals out of the wild. Then scientists can help them stay safe and have babies without dangers. Eventually, scientists release the animals back into the wild.

California condors were almost extinct in the wild. But scientists spent years doing captive breeding. Then

PEOPLE STILL PROTECT
CALIFORNIA CONDORS.

▼

Captive breeding helped Persian zebras.

they released the condors back into the wild. Their plan worked. The population rose, and California condors aren't close to going extinct anymore.

Captive breeding increases the number of animals in areas where they are endangered. Scientists are careful not to remove too many animals from the wild. If they remove too many animals, there might not be enough to keep that population going. Scientists also must make sure the animals they release don't have any diseases. If the animals are sick, they could harm the other animals.

Scientists make sure that animals raised in captivity know how to live in the wild. Then the animals will be able to find food and water. They will also know where they can find shelter.

A zoo is using captive breeding to grow the number of Sumatran tigers.

Chapter 4

STUDYING HABITATS

Researchers are learning more about animals and their habitats. These discoveries will help researchers know how to better protect them.

Protecting natural habitats is an important part of saving endangered species. Species with the smallest habitats are the most likely to be endangered. Some animals that live on islands or mountains are more likely to be endangered than animals that have more places they can live. Scientists are studying these environments to know how to protect them.

Scientists study animal habitats to learn more about them.

Using Data

Scientists collect a lot of data about animals' habitats. But using the data can be hard since scientists have so much information. Some scientists don't have enough space to store it. They can work with software developers to make using the data easier and more effective.

A scientist performs an experiment on invasive species to collect data.

THE WILDLIFE CONSERVATION NETWORK USES THIS DEVICE TO STORE THEIR DATA.

The Wildlife Conservation Network realized they could improve their data collection by using portable and high-capacity storage devices. Seagate, a leader in storage solutions, helped with data storage and cloud technologies. These resulted in easier and greater collaborations between scientists in the field.

Spotlight On
The Dian Fossey Gorilla Fund

Dian Fossey (*below*) worked to protect mountain gorillas in Rwanda. Mountain gorillas are still endangered. But there is hope. They live in east-central Africa. War, poaching, and humans moving into their territory have made life hard for the gorillas.

The Dian Fossey Gorilla Fund continues Fossey's work of protecting the mountain gorillas.

The Ellen DeGeneres Campus of the Dian Fossey Gorilla Fund in Rwanda is dedicated to research, education, and conservation. Because of the fund's work, the number of mountain gorillas is increasing.

You can make art to tell people about endangered animals.

Spread the Word

An important goal of fieldwork by scientists is to increase people's knowledge of what is being studied. Many conservation organizations spread the word about animals in danger. But you don't have to be an organization to do this. Kids can help too. You can learn more about an endangered animal and tell your friends and family members.

You can also help in other ways. Picking up litter is a great place to start. Trash can harm animals. It can destroy habitats, or animals might eat it and get sick. Always wear gloves and wash your hands after picking up litter. You can recycle at home or school too. This creates less trash that can harm animals. Every small action makes a difference. You have the power to help save animals!

With a grown-up, you can clean a park.

Save the Day

Captive breeding can be a great way to increase wild populations. But many scientists believe captive-born animals don't survive as well as those born and raised in the wild. What would you do to help captive-born animals gain the skills they need to survive in the wild?

Glossary

captivity: being kept in a place and not being able to leave

conservation: the protection of animals, plants, and other natural resources

data: the facts or information used to calculate, analyze, or plan something

environment: the natural world

extinct: no longer existing

habitat: the place where an animal naturally lives

poacher: someone who hunts or fishes illegally

population: the number of animals or people who live in a place

software: the programs that run on a computer and perform certain tasks

species: a group of animals that are similar and can produce babies together

Learn More

Bergin, Raymond. *Animals in Danger*. Minneapolis: Bearport, 2022.

Britannica Kids: Endangered Species
https://kids.britannica.com/kids/article/endangered-species/353099

Kids Can Save Animals
https://kidscansaveanimals.com

Kington, Emily. *Elephants*. Minneapolis: Hungry Tomato, 2022.

National Geographic Kids: Endangered Species Act
https://kids.nationalgeographic.com/history/article/endangered
-species-act

National Geographic Kids: Save Animals!
https://kids.nationalgeographic.com/nature/save-the-earth/article
/save-animals

Rossiter, Brienna. *Saving Earth's Animals*. Lake Elmo, MN: Focus Readers, 2022.

Walker, Tracy Sue. *Wildlife Conservation Technology*. Minneapolis: Lerner Publications, 2024.

Index

Photo Acknowledgments

Image credits: Fernan Archilla/Shutterstock, p. 5; CasarsaGuru/Getty Images, p. 6; Paul Souders/Getty Images, p. 7; AerialPerspective Works/Getty Images, p. 8; Dmitry Galaganov/ Shutterstock, p. 11; aappp/Shutterstock, p. 12; Eric VANDEVILLE/Gamma-Rapho/Getty Images, p. 14; Heiko Kiera/Shutterstock, p. 16; Vicki Jauron, Babylon and Beyond Photography/Getty Images, p. 17; Coolpicture/Getty Images p. 18; FRAYN/Shutterstock, p. 19; Sabih Jafri/Getty Images, p. 20; Ashok Kumar/500px/Getty Images, p. 21; Evgeny Haritonov/Shutterstock, p. 23; zaferkizilkaya/Shutterstock, p. 24; askirna/Shutterstock, p. 25; album/Alamy, p. 26; Alistair Berg/Getty Images, p. 27; Dmytro Zinkevych/Shutterstock, p. 28.

Cover: Chendongshan/Shutterstock.